Who Shot Goldilocks?

*How Alan Greenspan
did in our jobs, savings,
and retirement plans*

Who Shot Goldilocks?

*How Alan Greenspan
did in our jobs, savings,
and retirement plans*

William D. Rutherford

*to Steve
Best wishes*
[signature]
6/4/03

Crown Point Press USA
Portland, Oregon

Who Shot Goldilocks?

Copyright 2004 Crown Point Press USA

William D. Rutherford
www.whoshotgoldilocks.com

First Edition

Publisher's Cataloging-in-Publication

Rutherford, William, 1939-
    Who shot Goldilocks? : how Alan Greenspan did in
  our jobs, savings, and retirement plans /
  William Rutherford. -- 1st ed.
    p. cm.
    ISBN 0-9753104-0-2

    1. United States--Economic conditions--1981-2001.
    2. United States--Economic conditions--2001-   3. Greenspan, Alan,
  1926-   I. Title

  HC106.82.R88 2004   330.973'0929
                          QBI04-200172

Contents

The Goldilocks Economy –

the longest economic expansion

in post-war history –

not too hot…

not too cold…

just right!

Preface

Once upon a time...

The year was 1991, and John Q. Public was assessing his financial condition.

He, like the rest of the citizens of the United States, had just weathered a brief recession, much like the one he had endured in 1987. His finances were damaged, but he had survived. He still had his job, for which he was grateful, since many people his age had lost theirs and had only limited prospects for employment. He was able to put away some money for his retirement and for the college education of his 2.2 children. He was hopeful, even optimistic, about the future.

Little did he know what the next ten years would bring.

Over the next decade, he and his family would go on a wild ride in which their fortunes would soar and fall like a ride on the "Top thrill dragster," the highest rollercoaster in the world. As the U.S. economy continued to expand, John Q. Public's net worth, retirement savings, and tuition funds would increase along with it. Some called it the "wealth effect". Experts would call it the Goldilocks Economy, as it continued humming along at a comfortable pace, an economy that was not too hot so as to threaten inflation or too cool so as to inhibit growth. Like the porridge at the home of the three bears, it was *just right*. Soon, however, all of the "Goldilocks" economy's good work would be dashed; it would crash, and in such an enormous way that it would affect even the European and Asian economies.

The Goldilocks economy was not too hot and not too cold . . . just right!

John's paper net worth would be devastated along with his retirement and education funds. Millions of Americans would suffer the same fate, though that would be little comfort. His family's future, once so promising, was filled with uncertainty.

There has been much written about the economic rise of the 1990s, celebrating those who built up the U.S. economy. There even has been some explanation of the crash itself and its impact. But little has been written about *why* the burgeoning U.S. economy fell apart, and who bore the responsibilty. That is the aim of this book.

How could the world's largest economy suffer such a blow? How could its citizens be so devastated financially? What actions could have combined to create such a debacle? Who is responsible for the implosion of the world's most successful economy and our personal finances?

In short, who shot Goldilocks?

Chapter One:

Into the Woods

How we got here

The story of how the U.S. markets behaved during the great economic expansion of the 1990s really begins with a discussion of how the country and its markets behaved in the years leading up to that decade — starting, in fact, 30 years before.

It's no secret that the 1960s were a time of great social unrest in America, but they were also a time of great economic change, and chiefly for the same reasons: the Vietnam War and Lyndon Johnson's Great Society. The war in Vietnam, which took place over almost the entire decade, was a very expensive effort by itself, but in the middle of the decade Johnson initiated the package of social reforms he modeled on Franklin Delano Roosevelt's New Deal. It was a huge expansion of government and welfare programs.

When coupled with the money the government was spending in support of the war effort, there was suddenly a tremendous amount of money being released into the economy. This created a classic scenario for inflation.

Throughout the decade, as all that government spending energized the American economy, the financial markets rocketed up. It was an economy on steroids.

The Dow Jones Industrial Average hit the delirious high of 995.15 in February of 1966.

As inflation began to rise, the nation's central bank, the Federal Reserve, raised its key Federal Funds interest rate (the rate banks can charge each other for loans between banks) to try to contain it. By the time the Dow reached its December 1968 high of 985.21, the Fed had raised the Federal Funds rate to 6.3%, a 37% increase in a single year.

The effect was dramatic: By June of 1970, the Dow had collapsed to 631.16, losing over a third of its value.[1]

[1] See Chart One, pg. 91, for *Dow History*.

As the Dow fell, much personal wealth was destroyed; bankruptcies soared as bank after bank called their loans. Brokerage firms failed in staggering number, and people had no way to recover their money. Suicides rose. Clearly, drastic action was needed, and it came in the form of the Securities Investors Protection Act, through which Congress provided some backup funds to help ease investors' burdens in the event of future brokerage failures.

Reform was the response to crisis.

Economies are cyclical, of course, and by November of 1972, the markets had rallied. The Dow closed above 1000 for the first time ever that month — only to collapse to 577.60 two years later as a result of the OPEC oil embargo and the soaring price of oil.[2] Personal wealth was again destroyed; this time, pension funds were decimated, too. Congress responded again, with the Employment Retirement Income Security Act (ERISA). The price of oil thereafter became a central issue in foreign and domestic policy.

Again, reform followed crisis.

[2] See Chart Two, *Oil Prices 1970–2002*, pg. 92.

The equity and bond markets would suffer throughout the 1970s. Inflation had eroded the value of money, and made hard assets such as real estate more valuable. Gold bugs, fanatics whose belief that gold was the only investment that could hold its value in such an economy, popped up everywhere. Observers began to draw parallels between the U.S. economy and that of Weimar Germany, which had collapsed beneath runaway inflation. At the grocery store, price tags were overwritten daily to keep up with price increases. Interest rates soared.

A desperate President Nixon slapped on wage and price controls, only to create massive product shortages as manufacturers simply stopped making items for which they could not make a profit. Grocery stores had to call in police to stem riots when canning jars and lids arrived because housewives were trying to preserve food and cut the cost of feeding their families.

In 1976 the electorate, still reeling from the terrible economy and shocked by the Watergate scandal, turned south to Georgia Governor Jimmy Carter. President Carter wore his theology on his sleeve, which began a trend for American presidents that would endure and strengthen. He was also an engineer who couldn't let loose of details and delegate. Carter tried to manage every aspect of government, which was impossible for a President. By the end of his administration, he had lost control. American confidence in the economy continued to fall; international confidence in Carter and the U.S. plummeted, fueled by a failed rescue attempt, in April 1980, of U.S. hostages held in Iran. Meanwhile, interest rates spiraled nearly out of control. Home mortgage rates soared to 14%.

In 1980, the economy fell back into recession. Parts of the country experienced unemployment rates of 20% and higher, rates not seen since the Great Depression. In the financial markets, it seemed everyone suffered — equity holders, bondholders, even real estate suffered because of low occupancy. Working age people suffered greatly, even if they had a job.

Finally, late in 1980, the again disenchanted electorate chose former California Governor Ronald Reagan as the next U.S. President. His administration began with another sudden recession as Federal Reserve chairman Paul Volcker continued to raise interest rates further and tightened the money supply in an attempt to bring inflation under control. By June of 1981, just six months into Reagan's presidency, the Fed's key funds rate was a staggering 19.1%.[3] With the price of money so high, the economy stumbled once again.

Because of the slower economy, the demand for money was reduced and over time interest rates began to come down. Helped by a massive tax cut and massive deficits created by Reagan's supply-side economic strategy, the economy began to pick up.

Late in 1982, a full decade after it first hit 1000, the Dow crossed 1000 again.

By 1985, several structural changes had occurred. The U.S. was a debtor nation. We became dependent on foreign oil. Organized labor, after Reagan broke the national air traffic controllers strike, began to lose strength. Congress had begun to systematically get rid of regulation that adversely effected businesses. The massive computers of earlier years shrunk and were moved to desktops; a little known company called "Micro-Soft" developed an operating system for these computers, and the demand was insatiable. The economy grew more productive.

[3] See Chart Three, pg. 93.

As the economy progressed, the administration was given an opportunity to influence monetary policy: the term of Federal Reserve chairman Paul Volcker, a Democrat, was ending. A handpicked Fed chairman could help President Reagan set the course for continued economic strength. On August 11, 1987, after much back room dealing, Reagan appointed a Republican to replace Volcker. The nominee had an extensive career in government and business, and was a disciple of former Fed chair Arthur Burns. Reagan felt he would be a perfect fit.

His name was Alan Greenspan.

Chapter Two

The Cottage

The Federal Reserve and its Chairman

By 1987, when Greenspan took over its leadership, the Federal Reserve Bank had been in existence for nearly 75 years — that is, 75 years in its latest iteration. What we call the Fed, the nation's central bank, is in fact the fourth central bank in U.S. history.

Some historians claim the first central bank was formed in 1781 as the Bank of North America. This bank was patterned after the Bank of England. Predictably, the colonists wanted nothing to do with it, and it closed in 1790. (Thomas Jefferson, it should be noted, argued strenuously against the creation of a central bank on the grounds it violated the Constitution.) However, most historians agree that Congress created the first true central bank in 1791 at the urging of Alexander Hamilton after the collapse of the Bank of North America. This new central bank was called the First Bank of the United States. It was the largest corporation in the country and was dominated by big banking interests. America was then still a mainly agrarian nation, and many citizens were uncomfortable with the notion of a central bank, headquartered in "urban" Philadelphia. In 1811, when the bank's 20-year charter expired, Congress refused to renew it by a single vote.

Five years later Congress created a second central bank, which also only lasted a single 20-year period. Banking in the U.S. proceeded in a chaotic fashion, with many state banks issuing their own gold-backed currency. Then, just prior to the Civil War, Congress passed the National Banking Act. This created a standardized currency nationwide that was backed by U.S. government securities, which helped stabilize the economy but offered little help in the huge financial panics of 1893 and 1907. After J.P. Morgan bailed out Wall Street to help avert financial disaster in 1907, debate began again about creating a single central bank. This hotly contested debate finally ended six years later, when President Woodrow Wilson created yet another central bank when he signed the Federal Reserve Act of 1913.

Today's Fed is the result of the 1913 act. The most important purpose of the "Fed" is to set monetary policy — how much money is in circulation and the price of borrowing it.

The purpose of monetary policy is to support economic growth without undue inflation.

The Federal Reserve manages monetary policy by way of a series of decisions about the how big the nation's supply of money is, how easy it is to borrow, and the terms upon which it can be borrowed.

The Fed has several tools at its disposal to manage monetary policy, including the discount rate (the interest it charges banks that borrow from it) and reserve requirements (how much a bank must hold in reserves in relation to its deposits). Its most powerful tool is the federal funds rate, or the interest rate that banks charge each other for loans. The Fed announces a target rate, then manages this rate by buying and selling huge amounts of bonds through "open market" transactions, effectively raising or lowering the amount of money available to lend and therefore, the price of money.

Economists call the "neutral" rate of interest, the rate that neither stimulates the economy nor reins it in, allowing the economy to expand in line with its underlying productive potential.

The Fed is run by a board of seven governors, plus one representative from each of its 12 districts. Unfortunately, the geographic distinctions of those 12 districts are reflective of the economy in 1913. Only one board member is from the west (San Francisco), but two are from Missouri (Kansas City and St. Louis). The head of the board of Governors is the chairman of the Federal Reserve. Because of the enormous control this board exerts over the U.S. and ultimately the global economy, its chairman is one of the most powerful men in the world.

Alan Greenspan, the chairman of the Fed since his appointment by President Reagan in August of 1987, is as complex as he is powerful. His professional pedigree was outstanding. He'd held senior level economic positions under Presidents Nixon, Ford, Carter, and Reagan. He was senior advisor on economic activity at the Brookings Institute, and before that the CEO of Townsend-Greenspan, an economic consulting firm. He also has an interesting personal history that would come to explain many of his actions in the public eye during his time as chairman of the Fed.

Alan Greenspan was born in 1926 in New York City to Rose and Herbert Greenspan, who divorced when Alan was five. Alan and his mother moved in with her parents, and slept in their dining room.

Alan never developed a relationship with his absent father, a self-educated stock market analyst who published a book in 1936 called <u>The Recovery Ahead.</u> A year later, 1937, the market collapsed.

Herbert gave a copy of his book to his eight year old son, the inscription in the book he gave to Alan read: "May this my initial effort with a constant thought of you branch out into an endless chain of similar efforts so that at your maturity you may look back and endeavor to interpret the reasoning behind these logical forecasts and begin a like work of your own."

Perhaps the inscription was also a gift to Alan of the ability to communicate in obscure language, which left others in doubt as to what was being said. Greenspan's public and private utterances were so obscure that he proposed marriage to the woman that he had lived with for twelve years three times before she could understand what he was saying. Later his obfuscation would drive the financial markets mad.

Greenspan called his way of speaking "constructive ambiguity". Others called it "Fed speak". Reportedly, he practiced equivocation and giving long answers to questions.

After high school, where Alan became a master of baseball statistics rather than the sport itself, he attended the Institute of Musical Art (now Julliard), where he studied clarinet and piano. Afterward he traveled with the bebop-playing Henry Jerome Band before enrolling at New York University's graduate program in economics under the legendary Arthur Burns.

Burns taught that excess government spending caused inflation, and that government policies might actually be counter-productive to the economy. His textbooks preached a scientific approach to economics, which had to be built on data and observation.

Greenspan was taught never to commit to an idea unless it could be backed up by data.

His old friend Bob Kavesh, remarked "He (Greenspan) was the ultimate anatomist of the system"...nobody knew the numbers better than he did." In a way his approach could have been an alternative to his failed musical career. Both music and data can be seen as a progression toward a complete whole.

None of those around him thought he was destined for greatness. Even his former wife said she didn't see it coming. His old friends watched his career advance in utter amazement. He was viewed by some as Woody Allen with math skills. Still others thought him idiosyncratic and not well grounded in data. It was known that he read his data during his daily soak in the bathtub.

His obscure comments left him an easy exit from any position that he took and kept power in his hands since only he could really know what he was saying.

In the early 1950s, Greenspan and his first wife became acolytes of Ayn Rand, the Objectivist philosopher and author. Rand had suffered first hand with communism and was intensely supportive of capitalism. She was vehemently *laissez-faire*, and felt that Central Banks were destructive. She blamed the Great Depression on the Federal Reserve. The Objectivist view was that inflation is a form of taxation. Greenspan wrote for the *Objectivist* magazine in favor of the Gold standard as the only certain antidote to inflation. He criticized the Federal Reserve for its easy money policies. Rand's influence could be seen at Townsend-Greenspan, Greenspan's consulting firm, where there was an absolute rule that nothing could be published that might appear to advocate government interference in the economy. Indeed, deregulation was the preferred government policy.

Greenspan became a staunch supporter of limited government...

...and like Burns was extremely wary of inflation.

But, later, as Fed chairman, he would be responsible for <u>actively managing</u> the economy...

...to head off inflation — an activity his *laissez-faire* background suggests he was not entirely prepared for. Indeed, this could be seen in his first weeks on the job.

On the morning of August 18, 1987, one week after his appointment was finalized and he effectively took charge of the economy, Greenspan chaired his first Federal Reserve Open Market Committee (FOMC) meeting. The FOMC meets eight times a year to take the nation's economic pulse and formulate its monetary policy. Immediately, Greenspan voiced his concern that inflation was on the rise. At that time inflation stood at 3.7%, against a historical norm of 3.0%.[1] He urged the committee to raise the key Federal Funds rate in order to cool the economy. But the rest of the committee did not share Greenspan's concern. Perhaps his monotone, indirect approach

[1] See Charts Four and Five, pgs. 94-95.

was underwhelming; perhaps they did not see the evidence in the numbers that had convinced Greenspan. For whatever reason, the committee did not support him. Greenspan retreated.

Not for long, however. Greenspan, still convinced inflation was rising, set about to slow the economy with another tool at his disposal: the discount rate. The discount rate is the interest rate charged to commercial banks and other depository institutions on loans they receive from their regional Federal Reserve Bank's lending facility. The discount rate is set by the Fed's Board of Governors, not the FOMC, and since changes to the rate are made public, raising it would send a powerful message.

After that first FOMC meeting, Greenspan, no stranger to politics, lobbied the Board of Governors hard for a rate increase. Shortly thereafter, on September 4, the Board met in extraordinary circumstances. Two members were out of town, and there was one vacancy. With only four of seven members present, at Greenspan's urging, the Governors voted to raise the discount rate, the first rate increase in over three years.

The press announcement said the rate hike was to deal with potential inflation.

The market had been strong and there seemed to be little reason for this action. As the market digested this set of circumstances over the next few weeks, it did not like what it saw. Greenspan had run an end-around the FOMC, and took significant action more or less on his own.

Fear began to grip the markets. The week beginning October 12, 1987 was bad for the markets. That week saw a cumulative 235-point loss erasing $300 billion in value from corporate stocks. On Friday, October 16, the Dow sold down 108 points to punctuate the bad week. Also, by October 16, thirty year Treasury bond yields broke above 10%.[2] The yield had been 8.8% when Greenspan took office.

The following Monday October 19, 1987, the European markets opened to a wave of selling; by the time the U.S. markets opened, the U.S. markets were in free fall. By 11:30 AM, IBM stopped trading on the floor of the New York Stock Exchange because all orders were to sell. Before the day was over the stocks of many companies stopped trading. High-level discussions were held to suspend trading on all exchanges. Fear grew that the banking system and settlement

[2] See Chart Six, pg. 96.

system would seize up and fail. Howard Stone, a prominent specialist on the floor of the New York Stock exchange said," I owe so much money, I can't count it. This place (the stock exchange floor) is knee-deep in panic". By the close of the day, October 19, 1987, — a day that would come to be known as Black Monday — the Dow was down 508.32 points, or 22.6%.

For the first time ever, the market declined more than 20% in a single day.

By comparison the exchange had fallen 11.7 percent on Black Tuesday, October 29, 1929. Over one trillion dollars in value had disappeared, an amount greater than the Gross National Product of France. Warren Buffet lost $347 million, Bill Gates, $255 million, Sam Walton $1.75 billion. Thousands of people lost their jobs and their fortunes. This experience became known as the crash of '87.

Alan Greenspan had been Federal Reserve Chairman for 72 days.

Chapter Three

Who's been eating my porridge?

From Bush to Clinton

After eight years of Reagan, the U.S. economy was set to explode. One of the main reasons was that he had stared down the bad guys.

Reagan left many legacies, but none was more profound than the disintegration of the U.S.S.R.. His military buildup and foreign policy had outbid the "evil empire" in the high stakes game of the Cold War. Once the Berlin Wall fell and *glasnost* began, the world collected a "peace dividend" as global spending on arms and munitions fell dramatically. But more important, as capital was redirected toward peaceful purposes, world markets opened up for goods, services, and labor. Trade, construction, and travel all flourished.

This economic strength showed in the financial markets. The Dow rallied immediately after the crash of 1987, gaining 102.27 the very next day and 186.64 points two days later. Ironically, many felt that the quick comeback was due to the Federal Reserve's actions after Black Monday. Before trading began on October 20, the Fed issued this one-sentence statement: "The Federal Reserve, consistent with its responsibilities as the nation's central bank, affirmed today its readiness to serve as a source of liquidity to support the economic and financial system." Some saw this as leadership. In reality, Greenspan opposed making this statement — perhaps because of his *laissez faire* leanings — but eventually he did so, albeit grudgingly.

Many people were harmed by the Fed's dyspeptic moment. Jobs and fortunes were lost; the economy was rattled deeply. Still, the macro economy was strong enough to overcome the Fed's actions, and by the end of the Reagan era, the markets and economy had returned to an even keel. Markets were growing, productivity was increasing, profits were rising, and employment was strong.

Greenspan, however, was worried about the inflation that all this growth might cause. He began to react in late 1988, just after George H. W. Bush was elected President, by increasing the Federal Funds rate. In an FOMC meeting just weeks after Bush's inauguration in January of 1989, Greenspan said, "I frankly don't recall an economy that at least on the surface looks more balanced than the one we have." At the time, unemployment was 5.2%,[1] and inflation was 4.1%. Interest rates were 9%. Nevertheless, within two weeks, Greenspan raised rates twice, for a total of 3/4 %. By March 1989, the Federal Funds rate hit 9.85%.

By May, as a result of the rate increases, the economy was weakening. The Bush administration was concerned that the Fed had been too tight with interest rates, which might cause a recession.

Those same rate hikes had created a domino effect in the markets. Late in the summer of 1989, the high interest rate (junk) bond market collapsed, and on...

...Friday, October 13, the Dow fell 190 points — the biggest drop since the 1987 crash.

[1] See Chart Seven, pg. 97.

Greenspan felt the drop was unimportant, and did not act. He did not want to appear to be using the money supply to strengthen the market.

As a consequence of the collapse of the high yield bond market, the nation's savings and loans (institutions chartered to make home loans as opposed to commercial and personal loans like banks), which had loaded up on high interest bonds were severely impacted. As rates rose and the economy stalled, the value of the bonds plummeted. Many S&Ls were effectively broke.

The government was forced to bail them out. By the time it was over, the S&L debacle cost taxpayers billions of dollars to repair.

One lightening rod in the S&L crisis was a California concern called Lincoln Savings and Loan, which was led by Charles Keating. Greenspan had a problem. In 1984 Greenspan had lobbied in Washington on behalf of Keating.

In 1985, Greenspan wrote a letter to federal regulators stating that under Keating's leadership, Lincoln Savings and Loan had become "...a financially strong institution that presents no foreseeable risk."

In fact, Lincoln Savings and Loan Association was at the time engaged in a massive fraud, and its investments were nearly worthless. Greenspan reportedly was paid $12,000.00 for his services.

In the end, the takeover of Lincoln S&L alone would cost the taxpayers over $3 billion, and Keating would be convicted in state and Federal courts (later reversed) of fraud, racketeering and conspiracy.

Keating served four and one half years. Later, when Senator John McCain and four other senators came under investigation for helping Keating, McCain cited Greenspan's letter as one of the reasons he helped Keating with regulators. When he was criticized for his letter, Greenspan stated that he should not be responsible for views that he held two years earlier.

A short time later — in August of 1990, not long after the S&L disaster played out on the front pages of the world's newspapers — Saddam Hussein invaded Kuwait. The price of oil rose quickly to $30 per barrel. Since oil is priced in dollars per barrel, and the transaction amounts are very large, more dollars are needed in the available money supply to keep the capital markets "well lubricated." In a move guaranteed to make those necessary dollars scarce, however, the Federal Reserve kept a tight reign on the money supply. Once again, it feared inflation.

By November 1990 it was clear that the economy had grown worse. In addition, the nation's banks were hurting because of bad loans, particularly Latin American loans, and they were reluctant to loan more money to business. This created a credit crunch. Greenspan reluctantly agreed to a quarter point rate cut and a small loosening of the money supply.

These actions were too little and too late.

By December, the once-robust economy was in full recession. President Bush was forced to admit as much in a speech on January 2, 1991.

Shortly thereafter Operation Desert Storm commenced, and Iraq was defeated by February. In spite of the weak economy, President Bush enjoyed enormous popularity after the brief, efficient, and low-cost war. At one point his approval rating exceeded 90%.

Suddenly, Greenspan began to push for lower rates.

Some thought there was a connection between his interest in lower rates and his interest in his reappointment since his term was up for renewal in July.

By June, 1991, Fed data were showing improvement. At a June 30 meeting in the Oval Office with Bush and his economic advisors, Greenspan reported that there could be growth of 4-5% in the next quarter.

Ten days after this bullish report at the White House, Bush reappointed Greenspan as Federal Reserve Chairman.

Asked about the recession, Greenspan said, "I think it's a pretty safe bet at this stage to conclude that the decline is behind us and the outlook is continuing to improve."

He also found inflation "well contained," and made comments to that effect to Congress later that month.

However, Greenspan had never been known for his forecasting skills.

It's worth noting that for several years running, in its ranking of the inflation forecasts of major economists, the Federal Reserve had ranked Greenspan's firm Townsend-Greenspan dead last. In his initial confirmation hearing, in fact, Greenspan had been criticized by Wisconsin Senator William Proxmire for his "dismal" forecasting record.

Greenspan's strength had been in analyzing the economy, not forecasting.

His firm had overstated inflation forecasts by as much as 2.4%. (Journalist Barbara Walters, whom Greenspan once dated, has said that when it came to investing, she learned to do the *opposite* of what he recommended.)

With his forecasting record, it should come as no surprise that in the five months after Greenspan's comments, the economy took a nosedive.

Fearing inflation, the Fed kept a tight reign on the money supply. Unemployment increased to over 7%. In late October 1991, Greenspan told a business conference that the economy was "encountering headwinds." In December, the Board of Governors finally forced Greenspan into a 1% discount rate cut.

Bush and his economic advisors were increasingly unhappy with Greenspan, believing that his handling of the money supply was grossly inept. They wanted interest rate cuts. They labeled Greenspan as "a day late and a dollar short" and felt that he was allowing the economy to tank, and that it would take dramatic action to bring it back.

For his part Greenspan saw things differently. He felt the risk of inflation was too great. (The rate of inflation was 4.2% down from 5.4% in the preceding year.) The economy would have to grow on its own.

But it did not. By July 1992, the unemployment rate had risen alarmingly to 7.8%. The Federal Reserve responded with a 1/2% rate cut. This was followed in September by a 1/4% cut.

But the money supply moved little. The markets expected further easing, but Greenspan did not want market expectations to become self-fulfilling prophecies, so he delayed. Banks continued to be reluctant to lend.

By this time, Bush's reelection campaign was well underway. His general election opponent was Arkansas Governor Bill Clinton. Educated at Yale and Cambridge, Clinton was highly intelligent. His personal magnetism was renowned, and he could hold forth for hours on minute details of government policy. Still, he was given barely a chance against Bush, especially as he was repeatedly challenged about stories of his use of Arkansas state troopers as procurers of female companions.

But Clinton's brilliant, controversial campaign consultant, James Carville, had his finger on the pulse of the campaign. He seized upon the weakening economy as a campaign issue and relentlessly drove it home. Throughout Clinton's campaign offices Carville posted signs posted that read, "It's the economy, stupid." By the time his boss was nominated, the economy was well on its way to becoming the central issue.

Carville had help.

The Fed offered no further rate cuts before the election. The money supply barely budged. Not surprisingly, the economy went into recession. Unemployment rose to 7.0% on the eve of the election.

As more and more Americans found themselves out of work, the economy became the central point of the campaign. Bush's approval ratings tumbled.

On November 3, 1992, Clinton was elected President of the United States.

After the election, Greenspan finally agreed to cut interest rates and loosen, however slightly, the money supply. By the time Clinton took office, the recession was over.

As we will see later, Greenspan was to repeat his policy of curtailing the growth of the money supply in a period of rising oil prices, to the detriment of the capital markets.

Also he would again fail to provide interest rate relief in a timely manner. Greenspan's policies had been detrimental to the economy, and this time it cost one of our most popular presidents his job.

As Bush himself said, "I appointed him, and he disappointed me."

Greenspan did, however, manage to salvage his own job and retain his lofty standing: on the night of Clinton's first State of the Union address, Greenspan sat in the balcony between first lady Hillary Clinton and Tipper Gore, the wife of the vice president. The best seat in the house.

Chapter Four

Who's been sleeping in my bed?

The Goldilocks economy

President Clinton started his first term on shaky legs, but he did manage one remarkable feat: He got Congress to pass the biggest tax increase in our nation's history.

Many thought the nascent recovery would be pinched off by this government money grab, but remarkably, the economy had other things in mind. While few were looking, the economy was rediscovering technology. Industry was making things smaller, better, faster, and more productive. Companies could not ignore the efficiencies brought about by technology, and capital spending soared. It was a virtuous circle, more technology wrought more productivity, which yielded more profit, which yielded more capital available to buy more technology. Jobs were created. Tax revenues climbed. Inflation remained low as productivity rose. As profits, wages, and taxes rose, so did tax revenue, which led to a federal government surplus that helped stabilize interest rates.

The Goldilocks economy — the longest economic expansion in post-war history — was born. Not too hot, not too cold … just right!

Clinton's administration was bolstered by his decision to appoint Robert Rubin as an advisor on economic matters, and in 1995, as Secretary of the Treasury. Rubin, the former managing partner of Goldman Sachs, was mild mannered, self-effacing, and street wise. He brought his considerable knowledge of the world markets to the Treasury, which turned out to be our good fortune in a period that produced several remarkable crises that could have become far bigger problems. His sound advice to Clinton and Greenspan in the stormy times ahead helped keep the economy on a forward, if not even, trajectory.

Meanwhile, inflation remained Greenspan's paramount concern. In a speech to the Economic

Club of New York in April of 1993, Greenspan warned of the inflation premium he was seeing in bond yields, which he believed indicated that inflation would "significantly quicken" in the latter part of the '90s. "We need to be especially vigilant not to be mesmerized by the current tranquility of the inflation environment," he said. Still, he saw business expanding without an expansion in bank loans, an apparent contradiction. And he saw inventories declining as revenues increased, another contradiction. By 1994 he was convinced that though he could not detect inflation at that moment, it was surely just around the corner.

He relied on his data, but was apparently unaware that the economy had restructured itself.

Greenspan felt he needed to squash this looming inflation before it arrived, and elected to try a "soft landing," attempting to strike a balance between enough economic growth to avoid recession and little enough growth to avoid inflation. It is extremely difficult to achieve, and had never been done successfully.

To begin, he addressed interest rates. In January 1994, Greenspan testified before Congress that short-term rates were "abnormally low." The next month at the FOMC meeting, he said, "We are at the point where we finally have to start moving...We haven't raised interest rates in five years, which is in itself almost unimaginable." The Dow was about 4000, which he felt was too elevated. He requested and got a 1/4% rate increase from the FOMC. Furthermore, the FOMC agreed that for the first time in history, they would publicly announce a Fed Funds rate increase.

The rate increase was announced that day, February 4, 1994. By the end of the trading day, the Dow had suffered *its biggest loss in two years.*

Greenspan, however, was pleased. At the next several FOMC meetings he said that their actions helped break an emerging speculation in equities, and pricked a bubble in the bond market.

Over the course of the coming year, he continued to raise rates — in fact, doubling them from 3% to 6%. In testimony to Congress on February 22, 1995, Greenspan said the recent round of tightening had headed off inflation "not yet evident in the data" — meaning, not yet seen by anyone else.

President Clinton had a different perspective: He did not see the problem with strong economic growth and employment.

Clinton had wanted more money for more social programs, and Greenspan had wanted to reduce federal deficit. They'd agreed earlier they could do both by raising taxes, which Clinton did. Now that the economy was improving, Greenspan had decided that things were going too well, and pushed for interest rate increases.

Clinton was furious. Wasn't this the desired goal? What's wrong with prosperity? How can "too many" people be working?

On top of it all, long-term bond rates were shooting up. All of Clinton's efforts at deficit reduction had been for naught.

Clinton was right. As Greenspan pushed rate increases over the ensuing months, the economy stalled. Growth was an anemic 2% and unemployment was about 5.5%.

Clinton soon promoted Alan Blinder, a Princeton economist and member of the Council of Economic Advisors, to the post of Vice Chairman of the Fed. Clearly, he was grooming him to succeed Greenspan, whose term was drawing to a close. Greenspan distrusted Blinder — when a background check reported that Blinder wasn't a communist but was soft on inflation, Greenspan responded he'd have preferred him to be a communist — and froze him out of Fed operations, to the point Blinder left on his own several months later.

In spite of the slowing economy, and not wanting a battle with a fractious Republican Congress, President Clinton announced on February 22, 1996, that he would reappoint Greenspan to a third term as Chairman of the Federal Reserve. It wasn't much later in that election year that Greenspan decided on a cut in interest rates, and in November, Bill Clinton was reelected President.

—▪—

In the meantime, the global economy continued to grow.

This is worth noting because as the economy of the world became more connected, so did its currencies. However, there is evidence that the U.S. and the International Monetary Fund (IMF) didn't really understand how things were beginning to work in the global economy.

To begin with, in late 1994 and early 1995, Mexico endured a financial crisis that the U.S. resolved by lending the Mexican government $12.5 billion in high interest loans plus $20 billion from the Exchange Stabilization Fund. The U.S. didn't realize the precedent it was setting at the time.

Later, in July of 1997, Greenspan reported to Congress that prices were as stable as he had seen in the U.S., inflation was at bay and growth was strong.

That month, however, Thailand's currency, the baht, collapsed. And while it seemed like a minor event (Clinton dismissed the problems in Thailand as "a few glitches in the road"), it set off a chain of events that culminated with a currency crisis that would hit the U.S. several months later.

In August the Bangkok Bank of Commerce folded, followed by several property companies and Thai financial institutions. The Thai government was forced to defend the baht as money fled the country, but when the government reserves were exhausted, the Thai government had no other option than to let the baht float and therefore drop in value. The baht eventually lost 60% of its value, and the government closed 56 of the 58 largest financial institutions in Thailand.

While no one had been looking, it seems, U.S., Japanese, and European banks had lent nearly $700 billion to countries in Southeast Asia between 1993 and 1996. Growth was tremendous, and investment was seen as a solid bet in these rapidly developing countries. All this investment created a financial bubble, where expectations of returns were unaligned with how well the investments could perform. Thailand was the first casualty, but would not be the last.

Soon Malaysia and Indonesia were in trouble; the IMF was forced to offer the Philippines $1.1 billion in relief. Kia, a Korean carmaker, sought emergency assistance. The Hong Kong dollar, which was firmly pegged to the U.S. dollar, began to lag. Soon Korea was forced to defend its currency, which it did until its reserves were nearly exhausted. Massive intervention in financial markets by U.S. officials eventually slowed the Asian virus. But by the spring of 1998, another crisis emerged: Russia defaulted on its government bonds. Lending to countries such as Brazil and Argentina came to a halt.

That May, in 1998, Alan Greenspan visited President Clinton at the White House.

Apparently oblivious to the world economic crisis, Greenspan reported that we were in the *best economy that he had seen in 50 years.*

He noted that the economy should be showing signs of inflation, but was not. In fact we had the lowest rate of inflation since 1970.

But, on August 17, 1998, Russia devalued the ruble and suspended payment on its debt. The bond markets froze worldwide.

As the chill continued to grip global credit markets, one group in particular felt the effect: Long Term Capital Management (LTCM). LTCM was a hedge fund based in Westport, Connecticut, which had been organized by some very smart people, including two Nobel Prize-winning economists. Only those who could invest $10 million need apply to become clients. Its investment strategy was so complicated only a few claimed to understand it, but it keyed on movements in interest rates and amplifying their gains by the use of leverage (borrowing) – the more borrowing, the better.

By September, 1998, LTCM had over $1 trillion in leveraged funds, which were over 95% borrowed. If it failed, a worldwide crisis could follow. It stood to lose billions, and not just their client's money. In early September, LTCM's directors notified investors that they had lost $1.8 billion, or nearly half of its clients' capital. Furthermore, much of the portfolio could not be sold at all because the world bond market was in extremis.

What had started as a ripple in Thailand had grown into a tsunami in the world financial markets, and it was bearing down on the U.S.

Greenspan had previously assured Congress that there was no need to regulate funds like LTCM. His thesis was that professionals who knew what they were doing ran the funds — a statement eerily reminiscent of his assurances that Charles Keating would do an excellent job running Lincoln Savings & Loan. Now, it appeared they didn't know enough. On September 21, after an analysis of the LTCM books, a representative of the Federal Reserve concluded that if LTCM failed, there was a potential for a once-in-a-century meltdown. He thought there was a significant probability that the U.S. bond market would be wiped out for a week or a month, and after that no one could know what might happen.

As the markets opened in Asia the following day, knowledgeable investors smelled blood and sold out their positions. The next day, the chairman of the risk committee of Goldman Sachs called Greenspan to say that liquidity in the marketplace had evaporated, and that payments between financial institutions of hundreds of millions of dollars were due that evening, and might not be made. The Fed organized a hasty meeting of large banks and brokerage houses, and a bailout was finalized.

Afterward it was reported that Greenspan was unhappy. He felt that the probability that the world financial system would collapse was less than 50%, and that the Federal Reserve should not have lent its name or offices to the bailout. But it was done, and Greenspan had no choice but to back it.

It is interesting to speculate what might have happened if no deal had been arranged and LTCM had collapsed. Would Greenspan have been correct that there was less than a 50% chance of a worldwide market collapse? Perhaps even more interesting, why would one who had the power to prevent such a disaster let it happen, even if the chance of collapse was only 50%? Why run the risk given that so many would have suffered so much? If the captain of the Titanic had known there was an iceberg in his path, would he have stayed the course if the chance of collision was less than 50%? The answer can provide an insight into Greenspan's thinking and his tolerance for others to be hurt.

Chapter Five

Who broke my chair?
Irrational Exuberance

As the 1990s progressed, so did Alan Greenspan's celebrity.

The economy's continued strength, which was bolstered by advancements in technology, embellished his reputation. His handling of the 1997 Asian economic crisis elevated his stature further. The television show, A&E called him the most fascinating person of 1999. Internet sites devoted to him sprang up. CNBC showed him walking to every FOMC meeting, and even analyzed the thickness of his briefcase for possible clues to the outcome of the meeting.

As one of the most powerful men in the world, he could have been driven to the front door of those meetings, but he chose to walk for the cameras.

Greenspan clearly enjoyed his celebrity. He had courted several high-profile women in media, including NBC's Andrea Mitchell, whom he later married.

However, Greenspan will likely be remembered most for a single phrase and the reaction it caused.

At a December 5, 1996, American Enterprise Institute reception in his honor, Greenspan delivered a speech that was over 4,000 words long. This by itself was not uncommon, but about half way through, Greenspan did something that was unusual, and that only two other Federal Reserve chairmen had ever done before: He addressed the stock market directly.

He asked, "...[H]ow do we know when irrational exuberance has unduly escalated asset values, which then become subject to unexpected and prolonged contractions as they have in Japan over the last decade?"

Herbert Stein, Greenspan's predecessor at the Council of Economic Advisors, observed it was a good thing the U.S. markets were closed. But international markets that were already open immediately tumbled. The Nikkei had its biggest loss of the year. And, as more markets opened around the world, the sell off continued in its westward flow, until it washed up on the shores of the New York Stock Exchange.

At the opening bell the Dow was down 145 points. Greenspan's dramatic phrase was unprecedented for a Fed chairman.

Although the two previous market-addressing remarks had been mild (the 1929 and 1965 chairmen both expressed moderate concern about stock prices), Greenspan's dramatic phrase was an unmistakable shot across the bow of the market, and was seized on immediately by the international press. It was a theme he would return to later.

This comment cemented his move to a new realm, from Alan the Man to Greenspan the Myth. The cult of Greenspan was formed, and from then on his every word would be parsed. (Greenspan was aware of this; later, he would have a clerk monitor market movements during his congressional testimony.)

It also cemented his record as a terrible forecaster. Greenspan's strength had been in analyzing the economy, not forecasting. His comments to the AEI echoed similar ones he had made in a 1959 *Fortune* magazine article, where he warned of "overexuberance" in the S&P 500. In 1960, the following year, the market was up 43%. Remember, before he became chairman the Federal Reserve had ranked Greenspan's former firm, Townsend Greenspan, dead last in its ranking of inflation forecasters. In this instance, he proved his weakness once again:

The day following his comments to the AEI the Dow closed at 6448. The Dow would continue to climb and would not reach its peak until four years later.

A few short years later, as the economy was well on its way to a record 107 months of continuous growth, Greenspan would fall prey to his own irrational exuberance: Y2K.

From March of 1991 to the end of the decade, the Gross Domestic Product (GDP) grew at an average annual rate of 3.5%.[1] The Dow grew from 3,000 to over 10,000, and the NASDAQ from 500 to 5,000. Consumer confidence reached a record high of 144.7. Several hundred billion dollars were raised by companies in initial public offerings. A rising tide of tax dollars had outrun even the government's ability to spend, and the U.S. Budget moved into a surplus. Unemployment was below 4%. And though these unemployment and economic growth figures were both at levels that had historically signaled inflation, it remained low, in the 2-2.5% range, thanks largely to the increased productivity that technology made possible. Throw in several other factors — the end of the cold war and the subsequent reprioritizing of defense spending, free trade, low cost foreign goods and workers, the rush to the Internet, and a benign and supportive monetary policy — and it was easy to see why the economy was humming.

Greenspan agreed. In a speech on September 8, 1999, he said "…we are witnessing this decade in the United States, history's most compelling demonstration of free peoples operating in free markets."

[1] See Chart Eight, pg. 98.

But first there was one more matter to dispose of: the steady approach of January 1, 2000.

Many experts believed that as the dates on the world's computers turned over to the year 2000, or Y2K for short, those computers, most of which not been programmed to handle dates beyond 1999, would become confused and inoperative. It was widely feared that everything that depended upon a computer, from public utilities to ATMs to the federal government, would fail.

Consequently, panic ensued. U.S. companies spent billions in remediation. People withdrew money from banks and the stock market. In response, and to be sure that there was plenty of money in circulation, Greenspan's Fed began in September 1999 to increase the money supply dramatically.[2]

However, the Y2K problem turned out to be a big bore. Sensational predictions of civil unrest and martial law did not come to pass. At least one newspaper ran recipes for using up the Y2K emergency food horde. The defenders of the crisis said it was a big bore only because the Y2K bug was fixed, but they had a hard time explaining why countries that did little about Y2K — such as

[2] See Chart Nine, pg. 99.

Japan, China, Italy, and Venezuela — came through the "crisis" without a hitch. According to a World Bank survey, 33 developed countries did little to prepare for Y2K.

After Y2K, the flood of cash that Greenspan had infused into the money supply to solve the "bug" had to find a home. This additional money added fuel to the booming economy, exacerbating the "irrational exuberance" of the market. The 1920s had been called a "rich man's boom," but by 2000, half of U.S. households owned stock directly or through their retirement or pension plans and had benefited from the long economic expansion. This so-called "wealth effect" made people feel good, and they spent their money. The enhanced money supply also helped fuel the Internet and venture capital booms, creating a bubble. An economy on steroids—again.

Greenspan was worried. He was an analyzer of historical data, and was noted for poring over the 20,000+ indicators the Fed tracks. Some indicators come and go in importance, but he and the Fed were having a difficult time measuring the new economy, with productivity being particularly difficult to capture.

So, like a driver navigating his car while looking into the rear view mirror, Greenspan studiously relied on historical data for his decisions and once again failed to accurately forecast the future.

Fearful of the rising market he had helped to fuel, Greenspan announced that inflation was a threat even though there was none in sight. He was sure that inflation would become a threat because traditional economic theory held that it would in a situation like this one. And since the effect of productivity was difficult to capture, he was sure that inflation was at hand.[3] It was time to act. The Fed began a series of interest rate increases.

Since there was no evidence of inflation, Greenspan's comments and actions convinced Wall Street that he was targeting the market. He responded that he was targeting the effect that the markets were having on the economy, or the wealth effect. Greenspan reasoned that people had more money and if that money was chasing the same amount of goods, inflation was the

[3] See Chart Ten, pg. 100.

likely result. The rate increases would continue throughout 2000.

Thus began the unraveling of the greatest economy that the world had ever seen, and the beginning of the worst U.S bear market in seventy years.

Rising GDP, rising employment, rising profits, and rising productivity — it was all just too much to resist. It had to be fixed.

Chapter Six

Who Shot Goldilocks?
The End

At a March 6, 2000, conference in Boston, Chairman Greenspan gave a speech entitled, "The Revolution in Information Technology." He described with wonder a new age of productivity growth and transparency.

Previously, Greenspan said, business had a lagging knowledge of both customers' needs and the location of inventories and production materials that would satisfy them. Decisions were made from information that was hours and sometimes weeks old. Technological advances were changing that. The strong capital-spending boom showed that businesses continued to find and make a wide array of productivity enhancing investments in technology. "...And I see nothing," he said, "to suggest that these opportunities will peter out anytime soon."

Greenspan had finally recognized the transformative power of technology, the driver of the Goldilocks Economy. As in the case of his earlier economic predictions, his timing was remarkable: Ninety-six hours after his forecast, the NASDAQ began its descent.

The Fed would continue to raise interest rates for another nine months, raising them six times over the course of the year. When the inflation Greenspan forecast did not appear, he began to address the wealth effect, caused by the market increase, because he said it would cause inflation. Wall Street read his continued rate hikes as proof he was targeting the market. (Greenspan had said in a September 1996 FOMC meeting in Jackson Hole, Wyoming, that a way to curb the market would have been to raise margin requirements– but he said he didn't know what else it might do. Neither the Fed nor Greenspan have provided convincing evidence of why raising margin requirements would not have been effective if they were concerned about the run-up in the market.)

Additionally, to reverse the policy of pouring money into the economy in anticipation of Y2K, he began to drain money from the system. His timing could not have been worse. In a reprise of earlier failed policies, Greenspan tightened liquidity (between December 31, 1999, and December 31, 2000, he deleted $37 billion from the money supply [M1])[1] and raised interest rates, as the world price of oil was increasing from $10 to $37 per barrel. Because oil is priced in dollar contracts, and it takes an increasing supply of dollars when the price of oil increases, the Fed's tightening touched off a worldwide liquidity crisis, which the Fed should have recognized.[2]

Instead, intent on wringing excesses out of the market,the Fed kept on its tightening path until the markets hit the wall and left no skid marks.

By the end of 2000, the market was already nine months in to a steady decline. Over the two and a half years following Greenspan's Boston speech, U.S. stocks would lose fully half of their value — more than $8.5 trillion, equal to three quarters of the U.S.'s annual GDP. For much of that time, as he continued to act as cheerleader for the new economy, Greenspan had disregarded his own 1996 writing that criticized the 1929 Federal

[1] See Chart Nine pg. 99.
[2] See Chart Eleven, pg. 101.

Reserve for pumping up the economy prior to the October crash of that year.

The result was disastrous. In December of 2000, the stock market and the economy collapsed under the combined weight of the Federal Reserve's actions. Capital spending stopped almost instantly. Carly Fiorina, CEO of Hewlett Packard, later commented that, "in December, it was just like somebody turned off the lights." Sun Microsystems CEO Scott McNeely said, "we were going a 100 miles an hour, and then we weren't." CEO John Chambers of Cisco likened the crisis to a 500-year flood.

Chairman Greenspan, however, opined that the downturn had been "difficult to predict."

The minutes of the January 30-31, 2001, FOMC meeting showed that the Fed, despite all the evidence at their disposal, was truly surprised about the impact of their policies on the economy...

– that "the speed and extent of the slowdown were much more pronounced" than they'd expected. Weeks earlier, when it was clear that they had made a mistake, the Fed in a surprise inter-meeting move cut interest rates one-half percent. The rate cut caused the Dow to rally nearly 300 points, and the NASDAQ jumped 14% in one day. But the damage had been done. Capital spending stopped as companies reevaluated their revenue and profit projections. Business confidence was shattered. Orders were cancelled. Lay-offs began. At the January 30-31 meeting, the Fed, in full retreat, cut rates another one-half percent to, no avail.

The fourth quarter of 2000 saw one of the steepest market declines in history, and was followed by an even steeper decline in the first quarter of 2001.

The Federal Reserve had simply acted too aggressively in raising rates, and now was too timid in lowering them.

At some FOMC meetings it cut; at others, it did not. When one-half point reductions were indicated, it doled out one-quarter point cuts. Like a General sending reserves piecemeal into battle only to lose both the soldiers and the battle because he never committed enough force to affect the outcome, the Fed was too stingy. Its actions were once again, too little, and too late. Greenspan also ignored his own organization's research. The Fed, with 500 staff economists, commissioned a policy paper to determine the mistakes made by its Japanese counterpart after the property bubble burst in Japan in the 1990s.

The Fed concluded that the mistake of the Japanese central bank was to cut interest rates too little and too late.

© *Reprinted with special permission of North America Syndicate.*

Greenspan's Federal Reserve apparently decided to adopt — the "too little, too late" strategy that had failed in Japan, as its own.

The Fed continued its pattern of small interest rate cuts and slow monetary growth until September 11, 2001. After the terrorist attacks on the United States, it began a period of aggressive interest rate cuts. But even then, the Fed was not to be hurried. After the attacks, the stock market was closed for five days, and many wondered what the Fed would do when it reopened. As if to emphasize who was in charge, the Fed waited until the opening bell of the market to actually cut interest rates, and then by only one-half point. The Dow was down over 500 points that day. By week's end, the second-largest one-week market drop ever had occurred.

The Fed then began an "aggressive" program of interest rate cuts, but the shock of the attacks on the already weak economic system took its toll. As the economy weakened evidence of corporate scandals and greed also surfaced and had their effect. In the third quarter of 2001, the economy fell into recession, and the markets continued to decline for another year.

**By the end, in October 2002, we had
experienced the longest bear market in 70 years.
The market had declined for 32 months, three
times longer than the average bear market since
WWII and exceeded in history only by the Great
Depression's 34 months.**

For the period the Dow was down 37.8%, the
S&P was down 49.1%, and the NASDAQ was
down an astonishing 77.9%. Such notable blue
chips as AT&T (-76.6%), Ford Motor (-76.7%), and
Intel (-82.35%) were down drastically from their
peak. There was simply no place to hide in the
equity markets.

This was a Fed-caused downturn, and it was
unnecessary. Milton Friedman, Nobel winning
economist has taken the position that the Fed was
always wrong, "180 degrees wrong" and found a
strong correlation between tight money policy by
the Fed and the onset of recessions and depres-
sions.. MIT economist Rudi Dornbusch has said:"
None of the postwar expansions died of old age,
they were all murdered by the Fed. As CNBC's
Larry Kudlow put it, "The Fed had a senior
moment and completely lost their mind."

However, there was one bright spot: In September of 2002, Alan Greenspan became Sir Alan, knighted by the Queen of England "for his contribution to global economic stability."

Photo reprinted by permission of Allen Wastler, Managing Editor of CNN/Money and originally appeared on the CNN/Money website in an article in the "Wastler's Wanderings" column.

The trillions lost in the markets were not abstract numbers. It was not just the dot-comers and greedy Wall Street speculators who lost. The average investor lost as well.

Retirement dreams were dashed as pension and retirement funds were decimated. College dreams were put on hold as education funds were trashed. College and hospital endowments were smashed; the Shriners of North America had to close several of its Hospitals for crippled children because of investment losses. Even governments and schools suffered, as tax revenues declined sharply. In the business world, innovation was stifled in order to save money, and productivity gains were set back for years. No one knows how many innovative new companies with products for the improvement of the U.S. economy and its welfare were wiped out.

In a December 29, 2002, speech to the Economic Club of New York, Greenspan reported that the economy was going through a "soft spot."

"We thought it was a rough patch, but it turned out to be our life."

The New York Times reported that he was clearly worried about how history would view his tenure at the Fed.

The Federal Reserve under Alan Greenspan trod ground never walked on before by the Federal Reserve. America paid a huge price for Greenspan's policy of choking off rising prosperity under the aegis of fighting inflation. He repeated his pattern of seeing inflation when others did not, raising interest rates and curtailing the money supply to ward off that invisible inflation, to repeated disastrous consequences. From 2000-2002, the disaster was even more monumental. Just as he did at the time of the LTCM bailout, Greenspan demonstrated enormous capacity for allowing others to suffer.

Revenues, profits, margins and employment, all were rising without notable inflation. Still, Alan Greenspan could not resist "fixing" the Goldilocks Economy. We can all see how much better off we are for his efforts. The longest economic expansion is history is officially dead.

Who shot Goldilocks?
He is hiding in plain sight.

Afterward:

And they lived happily ever after...?

Between the market's high in March of 2000 and its low in October of 2002, $8.5 trillion in equity value disappeared. The market declined for 32 months, an event that had not occurred for seventy years. The effects of this loss in value are widespread, and felt by virtually everyone in America.

U.S. companies continue to struggle. Their costs continue to rise, but they have little pricing power. Over two million wage earners lost their jobs. Venture capital spending is a fraction of what it was before 2000. Retirement plans, school savings plans, and college and hospital endowments have suffered. And layoffs continue: As late as December of 2003, U.S. employers initiated 1,929 layoff events involving 192,633 workers.

People from all walks of life, not just investors, have been affected. Their futures have been altered dramatically, and usually for the worse. Alan Greenspan, however, has described this period as a "mild recession."

Recently, however, Greenspan has been sensitive to criticism of his handling of the economy. Concerned about his place in history, Greenspan has taken care to portray his role at the helm of the Federal Reserve as the earnest captain of a ship, not knowing what lay ahead but operating by the book. He has discounted the negative results of Fed actions, saying only that he trusts "that monetary policy has meaningfully contributed to the impressive performance of our economy in recent decades."

In a January 3, 2004, speech to the American Economic Association in San Diego, Greenspan took great pains to justify the Federal Reserve policies over his tenure. Practicing uncharacteristic humility, Greenspan conceded that making monetary policy is an "especially humbling activity," and that "uncertainty characterized virtually every meeting" of the FOMC during the crisis, and that the committee made decisions "we came to regret." He remarked that forecasting was elevated to "an even more prominent place in policy deliberations."Greenspan's comments were eerily reminiscent of those of Robert McNamara in the movie, "The Fog of War" who, when speaking of our Vietnam experience commented, "we made some mistakes."

The implications of Greenspan's speech are arresting.

He relied on historic economic data as a roadmap for the economy, and put faith in models he now concedes cannot capture the complexity of that economy and probably never will.

He studied his data, failed to properly forecast the future, and piloted the economy's ship right over a waterfall. Even now many worry that Greenspan has set the stage for a new asset bubble. In his testimony before Congress February 11 and 12, 2004, Greenspan gave scant comfort when he said, " Of particular importance to monetary policy makers is the possibility that our stance could become properly calibrated to evolving economic developments."

Given this apologia from the Federal Reserve chairman, what observations can we make?

Certainly we can conclude that the chairman is not as happy with his own performance as he professes; otherwise, he would not need to repeatedly justify his conduct.

We know from his history that he has a poor record as a forecaster. But isn't it a recipe for disaster to have one so confident yet inept at the helm? And how did it happen that a man elected by a single person, essentially responsible to no one, could achieve such power over the lives of millions of citizens, especially when that person sees his job as an   academic puzzle to solve rather than a series of real problems to real people? What can be done about this?

After previous market crisis, we have seen reform. Indeed, in the wake of corporate scandal in this cycle we have seen the Sarbanes-Oxley reforms. But why is it that reform never touches the Fed?

The Time for reform of the Federal Reserve is long overdue.

First, the legislative branch must do a better job of overseeing the actions of the chairman. Clearly, Greenspan has benefited from the politics of Washington; presidents have been forced to reappoint him, sometimes over their better judgment, because of gridlock between the executive and legislative branches. There is no easy way around a problem like this, but that does not excuse Congress from exercising proper oversight. For years the Chairman of the Federal Reserve has given testimony to Congress on the state of the economy under the Humphrey Hawkins Act. While this act has expired, the testimony continues, though informally. One effective way to begin such formalized oversight would be to make the act permanent so that the testimony continues.

Then there is the actual implementation of the act. Congress needs to be more rigorous in its questioning of the Chairman, so that both the elected representatives — and the people who elect them — can have a better understanding of what the Federal Reserve policies are. This is especially necessary when someone like Greenspan is in office, a man who rehearses giving obscure answers to questions. Congress should be less deferential and demand more.

Second, it is not asking too much for the Fed to communicate in plain English. Under the Greenspan administration, obfuscation has been made into an art form. It should be noted that the European Central Bank is not afraid to announce its rate decisions at a press conference at which questions can be asked.

Third, there should be a limit to how long one person can be Chairman of the Federal Reserve, just as there is for the presidency of the United States. Greenspan has been on the job since his appointment by Reagan in 1987. It is hard to believe that in this nation we could only find one person who could fill this position for such an extended period of time. Former Fed Chairman Marriner S. Eccles, who is widely considered the central bank's best leader, served 13 years, far less than Greenspan. Interestingly the Federal Reserve requires that its branch presidents retire at 65 years of age, but the Chairman is exempt. (Greenspan was 78 on March 6, 2004.) Thus, in addition to a length of service limit (less than the present 20 year limit), there should be an age limit.

Finally, the structure of the Federal Reserve should be reformed. When the current Federal Reserve System was established in 1913, the U.S. economy looked a great deal different than it does today. Then, the only branch west of Kansas City was placed in San Francisco, which fairly reflected the agrarian economy. Clearly this is not reflective of U.S. economy today. Newly redrawn districts could make a difference in the vote on the Federal Reserve. This recent debacle provides a good example. Technology, based largely in the Western U.S., drove the economy through the 1990s; when the Fed began its misguided policies, the Fed votes in favor of those policies were in the East and Midwest, whose economies had not dropped as hard as the tech driven west coast. Technology suffered mightily because of the effect of those policy changes. A Federal Reserve board that was more reflective of the real economy of the U.S. could give a more balanced approach to economic policy. (Remember: if it stood alone as a separate country, California would be the 5th largest economy in the world.) It should be noted that ten years ago, Microsoft, Dell, Cisco and Oracle employed a combined 29,778 people, but ten years later employed 168,750 – a net gain of 138,972 and a percentage gain of 467%. In contrast, in the same ten year period General Electric, General Motors, DuPont and Procter and Gamble lost over 400,000 jobs, or a loss of about one third of their jobs.

The economy is not just a statistic. The economy is the lives and fortunes of millions of individuals. The recent disaster shows what damage misguided, even if well intended, policies can cause. If the legislative and executive branches of government are interested in avoiding mistakes of the past, these policy recommendations would be a good place to start.

"Oh, I'm just riding out the cycle."

Snapshot

In early 2004, the U.S. economy began to recover from the hit it took in 2000-2002. The global economy also shows signs of recovering. But, the recovery is by no means universal. Signs of the recovery are strong in the U.S. and Asia, but less so in Europe. Published figures show Gross Domestic Product for the U.S. fourth quarter of 2003, up 4.1%. February's manufacturing index in the Midwest U.S. showed healthy growth, though down slightly from January, which had seen the fastest increase in nine years; but transportation orders fell 10.4%, the biggest decline since September 2002. The latter is especially worrying since transportation is often considered a good leading indicator. Consumer confidence declined sharply in February from January, and remained flat in March. Consumer optimism continues to wane. The price of oil exceeds $37.00 per barrel. Payrolls are expanding; however, unemployment numbers remain stubbornly high. The markets are a long way from recovering their losses.

Worries abound that the Federal Reserve, which has maintained very low interest rates for a sustained period, has created a new asset bubble, not only in the price of real estate, especially homes, but also in the equity markets which believe — once more — in the recovery. Having backed themselves into a corner by letting the crash get worse than necessary, the Fed has no choice but to keep interest rates low and hope the recovery follows. Hope, because it would be hard to lower rates from the current levels. The experience of Japan shows that low rates, by themselves, do not a recovery make. Should this be another bubble, the fallout will be enormous.

We also see the curious turn of Alan Greenspan, Chairman of the Board of the Federal Reserve, recently counseling homeowners on their choice of home mortgages. Odd, to say the least. Once again, he cheers on the bubble (if that is what it is, to paraphrase). He also points out that the Social Security system will be under funded by $7.5 trillion over the next 75 years. The reader may recall that this is about the same number by which the market declined between 2000 and 2002. Of course these numbers are not coincident, but they are coincidental. And, you never hear Greenspan mention that the price of oil hovers near $40 bbl, and the impact that will have on the economy. Some say that Greenspan, realizing that he is approaching the end of his career, wants to get all his ideas on the table. Others think that he is diverting attention from the problems that he brought about.

The economic numbers have to be worrisome to President George W. Bush and his supporters. The question is, will Greenspan send yet another Bush into retirement?

As always, the American economy with its incredible ability to innovate will survive and prosper. That said, economic power is shifting. The price of oil is rising and our dependence continues and increases. Forty percent of our debt is in foreign hands, in a Faustian bargain that allows us to buy foreign goods so long as they loan us the money. Federal deficits rise, putting upward pressure on long-term interest rates, which is detrimental to the economy. And Asia, especially China, is becoming a greater economic power. With lower labor rates and absence of the health care costs in overseas markets, many jobs are being sent offshore. Outsourcing of jobs to Asia and India is sure to be an issue in the forthcoming Presidential campaign.

It is reported that Greenspan looks at 20,000 data points to arrive at his conclusions. These data points are all by definition history, some old and some no doubt inaccurate. In his speech on January 3, 2004, he admitted that the Fed models don't work and may never work. It is reminiscent of the Russian apparatchiks who attempted to set prices for goods in their command economy. With so may prices to be set, it just couldn't work. We are using thousands of historical data points, in models that don't work, to make predictions.

There should be a better way.

Acknowledgments

A Word on the Text

In writing this book, it was not possible to have face-to-face interviews; therefore, I have relied almost exclusively on previously published information.

There is a voluminous amount of data on the U.S. economy that is available publicly, as is information about the history of the Federal Reserve. In fact, much of the information I have used came from the Fed's own website, including the minutes of its meetings. I have also relied upon historical market information published by Dow Jones, Standard & Poor, Value Line and my good friends at GaveKal. I have also relied on published news reports from various publications both print and Internet.

I have also relied on the vast research of other authors who have written extensively and well about Alan Greenspan. Justin Martin's *Greenspan:*

The Man Behind the Money (Cambridge: Perseus Publishing, 2000) and Bob Woodward's *Maestro: Greenspan's Fed and the American Boom* (New York: Simon & Shuster, 2000) are excellent studies of the man and his place in history, and have been indispensable. David B. Sicilia and Jeffrey L. Cruikshank's *The Greenspan Effect: Words that Move the World's Markets* (New York: McGraw-Hill, 2000) was of singular help in gauging how the rest of the world receives Greenspan and reacts to him. Finally, Clyde Prestowitz's superb *Rogue Nation: American Unilateralism and the Failure of Good Intentions* (New York: Basic Books, 2003) lays out in lucid detail how the Federal Reserve's actions ripple through the global economy.

There are many useful websites for the review of Fed policy; a place to begin is fmccenter.org

Without these works, I could not have written this book. Any fault of fact or reason within these pages has no bearing on the work of these men. It is entirely mine.

– *W.D.R., April 2004*

Thank You

Many people aided and encouraged me in the writing of this book. My editor Greg Netzer did a marvelous job of organizing my thoughts and making a readable text. Jim Ulatowski did valiant work as researcher and was indispensable to the success of this book. I received valuable assistance from Lynda Falkenstein, "the Niche Doctor", and Anita Jones, who was responsible for layout and jacket design.

My patient and understanding wife Karen Anderegg deserves much credit. Comments from pre-publication readers such as Wayne Rutherford, Jackson Lewis, and Brenda Peterson were also helpful.

Author with Mike Mansfield, former Senate Majority Leader (Dem.) and U.S. Ambassador to Japan, following economic briefing by Mansfield and his staff in Tokyo, 1987.

About the Author

William D. Rutherford is President of Rutherford Investment Management LLC. A graduate of Harvard Law School, Rutherford has been on the board of numerous U.S. and international corporations and the CEO or president of two international investment companies with offices in New York City, London, Paris, Tokyo and Frankfurt. Mr. Rutherford has been the Treasurer of the State of Oregon and chair of the Oregon Investment Council overseeing $14 Billion in investment funds. He has appeared on CNBC and Bloomberg television, and quoted in the *New York Times*, *Wall Street Journal*, *Business Week*, and other publications. Honors include listings in *Who's Who in America* and *Who's Who in the World*.

Appendix

Chart One: Dow Jones Industrial Average:
                1945–2003

Chart Two: Oil Prices: 1970–2002

Chart Three: Federal Funds Rate: 1970–2003

Chart Four: Annual Rate of Inflation: 1970–2003

Chart Five: CPI, Cumulation: 1945–2003

Chart Six: Treasury Bond Yields: 1977–2002

Chart Seven: Unemployment Rate: 1948–2003

Chart Eight: Gross Domestic Product Annual
                Percentage Change: 1930–2003

Chart Nine: Money Supply (M1) in $ Billions:
                1999–2001

Chart Ten: Productivity % of Change: 1990–2003

Chart Eleven: Drain on Global Liquidity Caused
                by Oil: 1984–2004

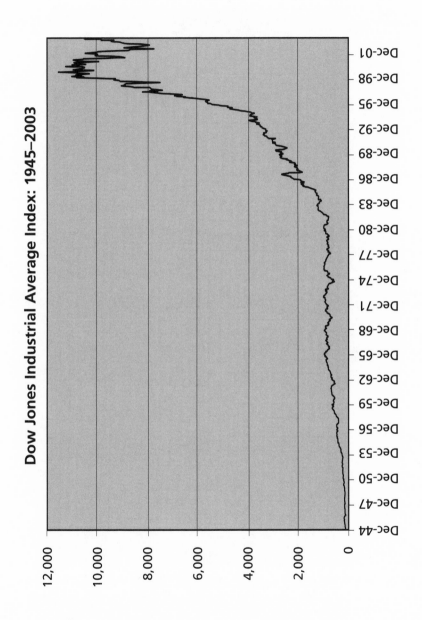

Dow Jones Industrial Average Index: 1945–2003

Chart Two

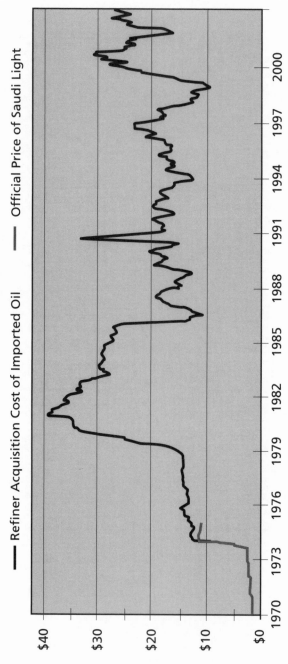

Oil Prices: 1970–2002

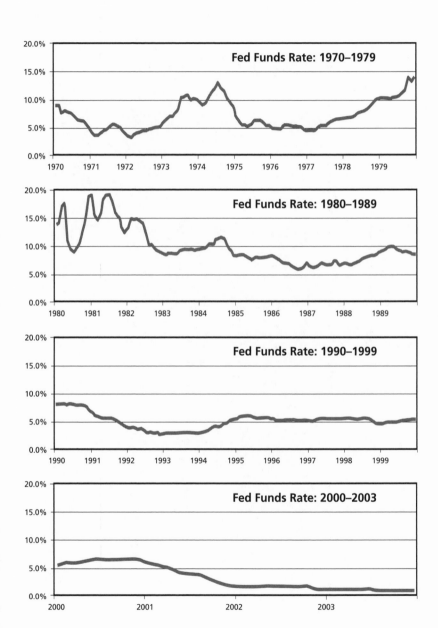

Chart Four

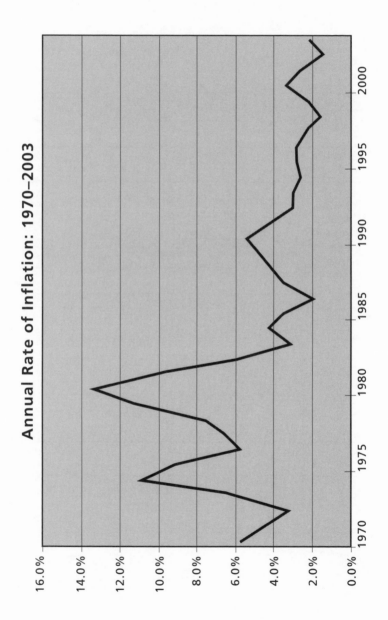

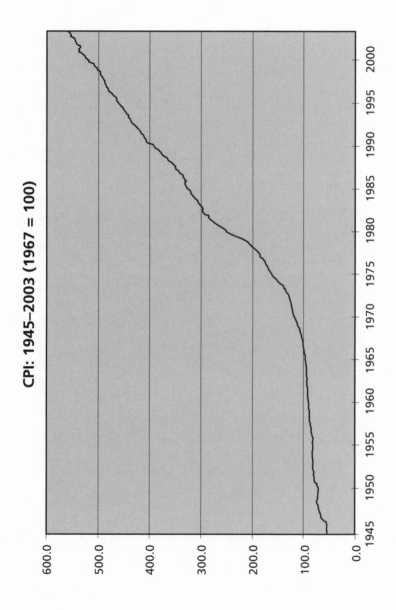

CPI: 1945–2003 (1967 = 100)

Chart Six

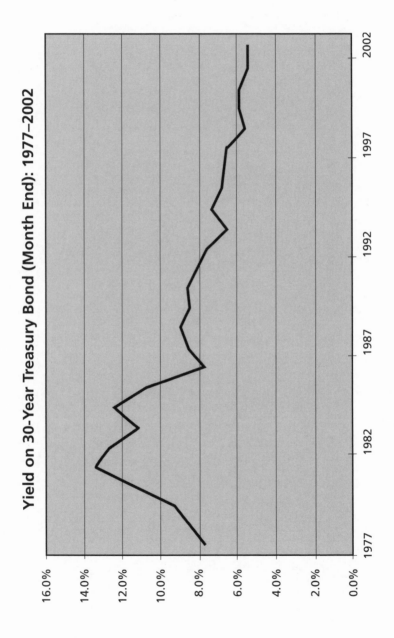

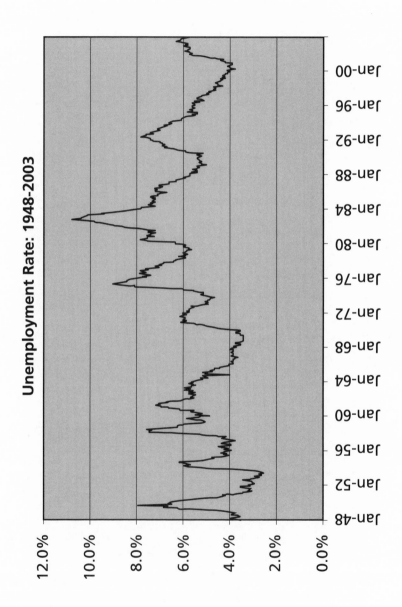

Unemployment Rate: 1948-2003

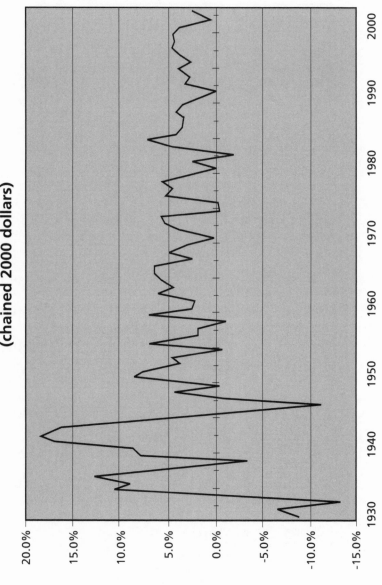

GDP Annual Percent Change: 1930–2003 (chained 2000 dollars)

Seasonally Adjusted Money Supply (M1) in Billions of Dollars: 1999–2001

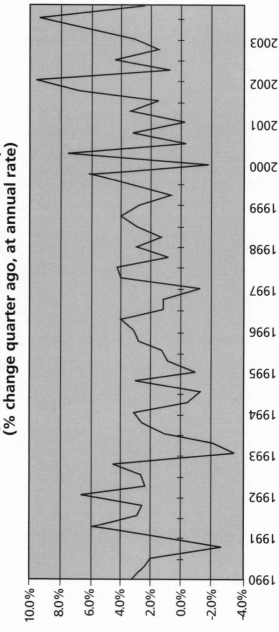

Productivity 1990–2003: Non-farm Business Output PerHour
(% change quarter ago, at annual rate)

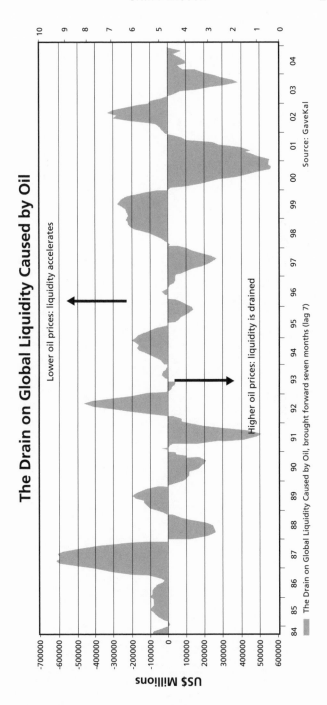

The Drain on Global Liquidity Caused by Oil

ORDER FORM

for additional copies of *Who Shot Goldilocks?*

Detach and mail this form with your check
or fax with your credit card number.

Please send me_____ copies @ **$18.95**
plus **$4.95** for shipping one copy, plus **$1.00** for
each additional copy to the same address.

❑   Check enclosed
❑   Charge my credit card
❑   VISA   ❑   Mastercard

Card Number   _____

Expiration date_____

Signature   _____

Name _____

Address _____

City_____

State_____ Zip _____

Email _____

Mail to above address ❑   Different address ❑

Please provide:

_____

_____

Total books ____ **plus** ____ **for shipping =** _____

For more than 10 copies call:
Toll Free: 1-888-755-6546

Mail to: Crown Point Press USA
10300 SW Greenburg Rd., Suite 115, Portland, OR 97223

Fax to: 503-452-0120

www.whoshotgoldilocks.com